THE ADMIRATIONS

The Admirations

poems by
Lex Runciman

LHP

ACKNOWLEDGMENTS

Grateful acknowledgment is made to the editors of the magazines in which the following poems (some in earlier versions) first appeared:

Calapooya Collage "1492 Fremont"
The Chariton Review "Family Albums," "Touring Arizona"
College English "Furniture," "Jerome, Arizona," "Fairmoor"
The Cumberland Poetry Review "Arrival"
Cutbank "Grosbeaks"
Hubbub "Before Sleep," "Harbor," "Indulgence," "July at the 45th Parallel"
Intro 10 "Robert Frost"
The Minnesota Review "Waiting for Nothing"
The Missouri Review "Repititions"
Northwest Review "December 7"
Oregon East "Parochial"
Oregon English "Blue," "Faces"
Ploughshares "The Biographer's Art"
Quarterly West "Postcard"
Scratchgravel Hills "Child"
The Seattle Review "All Day the Sea" (previously titled "West")
The Slackwater Review "Viewers," "Vermeer: The Music Lesson"
Willow Springs "Zuelke's" (previously titled "Vacation")

"Walkers" is reprinted by permission from *The New England Review & Bread Loaf Quarterly*, Vol. VII, Number 3 (Spring, 1985). Copyright by Lex Runciman.

"Furniture" also appeared in the 1985 edition of the *Anthology of Magazine Verse & Yearbook of American Poetry*.

"Postcard" and "Arrival" also appeared in *Old Mail*, a limited edition chapbook printed by Carol Williams at the Gandeamus Press.

———————————

Design by Christopher Howell and Barbara Anderson
Cover Art by Harry Fox

Publication of this book was made possible in part by a grant from the Oregon Arts Commission.

———————————

Library of Congress Cataloging in Publication Data

Runciman, Lex.
  The admirations

  I. Title
  PS3568.U465A7 1989   811'.54--dc19   88-31219

ISBN 0-89924-061-5 paper
      0-89924-062-3 cloth

Lynx House Press books are distributed by Small Press Distribution, 1814 San Pablo Avenue, Berkeley, California 94702.

———————————

Lynx House Press, Box 640, Amherst, Massachusetts 01004

For Elizabeth Helen and Jane Christine
For their mother

And in memory of
Geneva Helen Runciman

Contents

The Biographer's Art

Walkers

Faces

Faces

Everyone believes it.
I looked at him as he spoke:
streaked hair, his face
pale, dripping wet, and as present to me then
as a lover's or a killer's.
Whatever you call it, nuclear
winter, our drift towards disaster.
His hands rose from his lap.
Meaning, I'm talking about.
Progress, something inevitable as sin.
Friday morning. He was smiling
as he said all this. I was smiling.

'Course it's horrible
to contemplate, horrible…the deaths…
mother and father, brother and sister,
ashes. As if he
was trying on a new word. Ashes.

Hats off, raincoats
unbuckled or unbuttoned,
the other bus passengers sat
or stood in the narrow aisle,
their heads turned towards us then
not because they had heard him
(he'd spoken barely above a whisper),
but because he had begun
to sob, bent over at the waist,
keening, rocking in the seat.
A wail—it was, suddenly,
the only sound. Then a woman's voice:
Why, he's sobbing like a baby…

I shrugged my shoulders,
mouthed the truth at them
—*I don't know this man.*

After that, we just listened

to this adult stranger weeping
on my knees now, on my
briefcase and raincoat.
I rubbed my hand over the fogged glass.
Below us, the bus tires
hissed on wet pavement.
Ahead, I could see my stop:
same matronly woman
and a child watching the doors
approach and slow, their faces
sleepy under hooded jackets.

Repetitions

A truck motors down our hill,
sun on its windshield, a white, rusted hood.
I glance at it and its anonymous driver.
The time must be earliest spring
                          or late autumn—
long shadows, and no leaves on maples.
The truck turns our corner and goes on

and there, flat on the pavement,
                          is my daughter.
Even as the truck passes over her, she is screaming
and I have never heard such terror.
She wears a white shirt. She screams
and stands, red stains widening as she runs toward me.
There is a look on her face ...

Dream, I say to myself,
to ignore the tears, her terror, my own
mortal panic. Dream. Dream. And
if she runs, it must be she survives.
But what I see is her body, arms outstretched,
a reddening shirt,
                    an open, bloody mouth.
As she runs toward me, I wake.

Rational, calm,
           I'd say dreams
carry their curious meanings like music.
When I wake crazy out of that vision,
I want only to order her mother: never dress her
in a white shirt. I want to instruct all daughters
with a permanent, terrifying intensity,

don't play in any street ever.
I want to abandon this house.
                  Instead, rational,
I write out the dreams on paper folded in thirds
and burn it. Ink curls and is ash.
I write it again here to ridicule my fear.
What a strange, disturbing dream,

says my reasonable self, before it goes upstairs,
before it brushes its teeth and avoids the mirror,
before it looks in on my sleeping daughters
and finds them as they are,
                  the regular,
hushed respirations. Rain falls like pebbles.
Face, and face. Name, and another name.

Field

It's summer.
I'm in the field, chasing insects
to keep them airborne, or at least moving
so I cannot see those bulging multiple eyes
above the moveable mouthparts. When I get tired,
there's always milkweed to snap (the milk
rises like frothy steam), always rocks to throw,
a whole landscape of targets. Once
I found a cordovan oxford cracking in heat.
A sad murderer left it in his timely haste.
I found a ribbon dropped by the murderer's
virtuous lover, a woman who prays rosaries
and keeps their bedroom door locked as tight
as our gun case. Cats come here. Adults
wheel full barrels of lawn clippings, raked
leaves and bush and tree prunings.
Some dismembered branches wave for weeks,
pale and dying. Two stunted apple trees
have rooted in the ancient grass.
Two hollow televisions peel their layered
veneers. Sometimes in bed, restless
because the air is warm and the sun
isn't even down, I pretend I live out there
all my life, permanent burrs on my socks.
I lie back imagining clouds and what they
think of sky, imagining birds
and what they think of clouds.

Robert Frost

But for pictures
and the memory-twisted reminiscences
of younger men,
I never knew him.
I know when he died, 1963
the day after my father's birthday.
I was twelve and remember
reading the dying
newspaper tribute.
And I remember one day,
January, his standing
in the black box of our television,
holding a paper
gone suddenly white
and silent in cold sun.
So he put it down
and began reciting
The Gift Outright
into the clear air, a public man
talking the way I believed a private man
would talk, if he ever did.

Viewers

Up thin steps, past
careful italic script
painted on the wire-reinforced glass,
at the top of a burnished mahogany railing,
scant weeks ago, without ceremony
the local television museum opened its door.
Now the second storey battleship linoleum
of a former dentist's waiting room
shines, reflected rows of sunlight
between the rows of vacant carrells—
gray boxes, headphones, empty chairs.
Behind a counter like a bank teller's
an already bored attendant takes all orders,
assigning the number of an unused screen.
Drunks and the other aimless
haven't found this place yet.
They will, and request I Love Lucy,
The Untouchables, The Fugitive.
One man only slightly overflowing his chair
is watching Jack Paar, the old
Tonight shows. Another watches commercials,
look sharp, feel sharp, be sharp—
the Gillette song singing on his lips.
One screen won't let you go, a building
you have seen before, the Texas School
Depository, and there is the motorcade,
Lee Harvey Oswald blown backwards
clutching his middle. How many times
did you see it that afternoon, three
times, four? There is the funeral cortege,
a windy day, the silence of the living room
unbroken as you wish again your parents

might explain, and they don't, no school,
your father inexplicably home, the streets
outside empty, and inside no one
looking at anyone else's face.
The woman wearing the headphones
is weeping. It occurs to you
all she has not requested.
She has not noticed
you too have been watching.

Narrative

After uneasy dinner,
After parking in the tiered employee garage
Empty at that hour, stepping over
Muddied construction plywood—
Sewer, water, gas, phone,
Something unburied under there—the rain
Quit at that moment, all clouds
In visible hurry, dark against dark,
The scanner doors opening:

Admissions, billing, the empty
Spacious lobby, philodendron alive,
Philodendron waxy, paintings,
Anything, Muzak, as the Otis
Elevator doors close, and we rise.

In the Third Floor Intensive Care
Waiting Area, there's a closet for coats,
Four black bent wire hangars on a wooden dowel.
The television's off. A rawboned man,
Maybe 50, hair combed once, earlier,
Sits as though his chair, any chair,
Is foreign. His son, daughter,
Sister—whoever it is—cannot,
He has been told via a speaker,
Cannot see him now.

Nothing's ordered. My brother's here.

No, not here, still three floors
Above us, dreaming his white dream

As women and men, all strangers
In odd billowy clothes,
Excise the tumor that chokes him.
Go *home*, we're told. *Hours yet*,
And, *We'll call*.... Go home,
As though we have choices, choose.

11

Before Sleep

Sleepless, dully animal,
we walked the bare night corridors,
stood idly at tall windows
observing the progress of a wan December sun
in no hurry to lift itself
over frozen mountains,
the geometry of streetlamps going out.

Gradually as the day arrived,
your labors took us beyond conversation
for minutes at a time,
minutes meaning nothing,
whatever we had said picked up again
casually, and strung out again
in the waiting.

Possessed with the idea,
now the body's one continuing fact,
you worked that night, that morning,
finally beyond all rational love,
alone, for what we both wanted.
In that room I think only the ceiling tiles,
those damped acoustical squares, were calm.

Then all waiting sloughed like a skin,
time found us adrenalin-awake
in the clean room, light condensing
off every stainless object. There
we follow the outline of health,
the separate, difficult events.
And one moment the scrubbed air

is vacant. And one moment it carries
its original, at last audible voice
rising as fragile as a bubble,
not angry, rising like a question,
one statement, a chorus of surprise.
Now the old, literate life is over.
Our unspoken life begins.

Grosbeaks

I say I don't know where
they come from,

as from the screendoor
we watch the migrant underwings
of grosbeaks, a huge sheet of wings:
the choreography of one instinct
and one sound as they light
simultaneous in our tree.

At her age, a shoe is an equal
in conversation, still unsure
which things
answer, or stay unconsciously mute,
the rude gloves, which, though spoken to,
do not move or speak,
not even when she chews them.

I stand in the doorway
holding her, both of us
listening to this score of strangers
chittering and beaking
invisibly in the elm,

when she lets out
an unholy, animal yell
and I almost drop her—
the whole world
flying up in our faces.

December 7

Asleep, half drunk in uniform,
noise woke me: shoes,
the clangor of ship bells,
then the *Missouri*,—a hollow-bellied
thunderclap that knocked me to the bulkhead.
On deck I thought about God.

Leaves gone
white under early storm,
my parents waited,
living the anonymous numbers
of dead and wounded—six days
for my postcard to arrive.

I had not thought of that in years.

Fire. Voices twisted by fire.
One smell that even now spoils meals.
Faces, dreams I once
feared more than death—they
persist. They say remember

a blank moon,
and the tide rocking, harbor lights
on the surface like oil,
the smell of warm beer,
a distant radio
playing young Benny Goodman.

Nostalgia

to them change never comes; neither the change
of seasons nor of sorrows
                    —*Melville*

Always it is late. The crickets,
Of course, sing. Chairs,
Chairs refuse no one. A single lamp
Burns its tungsten wire under a linen shade.

Anger is what you possess, the futile,
Bitter complement of nothing.
A photographed face, four photographed faces:
One adult male, moustache; one adult female,
Brunette under box hat; two male children,
One of whom claims as truth, as simple truth
He is your father. He is your father
And the photograph belongs truly to him,
To his era.

            Of the four figures,
The two youngest are now old men. The adults
Recline in spotless ultimate files.

Beyond the dark window, crickets resume.
Or it is winter, fields white,
Sparse traffic in low gear.....

Steady as electricity,
The photographed figures exist
Beyond imagining, not quite beyond it.
They have landed on a dock long since decayed.
That is their luggage—two trunks.
They see a photographer and recognize
An impulse to record this moment.
Even as they arrange themselves to be still,
They have no idea where they are.

1970, Santa Clara, Reading the Names

Where shall we live? For our lives are not lived
—Randall Jarrell

Ignoring parked cars, the colored
Fountain lights making water
The pastel illusion of rose;
Ignoring lazy palm fronds, the continuous
Splash, and how a voice, his, came back
Flat off the brick face of a dormitory,
He began to read.
                People watched,
Listened for a moment, their unmoved shoes
Staying or leaving; birds, juncoes maybe,
Flew at the edges of vision, in the silk trees,
The mimosa; miles overhead, twin contrails
Widened in the high wind, white on blue—
Nothing altered the names, American
Consonants and vowels: name,
Town, state, the best absolutely strange:
Bardstown or Beallsville or Vacant City, Florida.

He read for his hour, finished
Startled at the fact of his standing there,
Time gone, the new reader,
A woman tucking long hair behind her ear,
Beginning exactly where, on the list,
He'd pointed his finger....
He read for his hour, lost,
Entirely lost by the end of it,
In the failures of what names mean,
Their rhythms, and sweet incantations.

Family Albums

Children! Children! form the point of all.
Children & high art.
—*John Berryman*

Thick between imitation brown leather
Reside our random, prosaic lives:
Illusion. No illness, no petty indulgence,
No stupid anger.

Who remembers infancy?
Our children confuse theirs,
The times, the towns, the furniture
Cheap, ugly to begin with, and with only joy
Sold later out of a drafty garage.
In all its drab, irregular color,
Here is the pitiable daybed, the one
Our children believe they remember.
And they believe they did indeed sleep
There, in those houses, those footed pajamas,
And played with recognizable friends,
Faces unchanging though their real names
Escape us—when they surface
In conversational dreams, we name them,
Facts we take time to invent.

Here we are learning to walk.
Here we are smooth, naked, and three.
Here is our silly garden, a sad, thin line
Of carrots...

In the cliche outside,
Crocus bloom thinner than paper.
We've no pictures for this:
Sky's uncertain blue.
The neighbor's dead oaks rouse.
Italian plums bud like a new disease.
Our children still love their lives.

Fairmoor

Jerome, Arizona

I have been there,
plastic flowers rosy on the sill,
one dead shoe on the decrepit porch,
that mountain of green slag
not the sum of anyone's life,
not mine or yours.
Years ago vases sailed through these windows.
Here is a cracked banister, the dead
spires of roses...

This is the sadness
of history, and I come here
again and again
to feel this way, almost joy,
the moon so beautiful
it must be Chinese.

Touring Arizona

Along a dry canyon wash,
sago-lilies and vermillion
reclaim the Hohokam canals.
Pond bottoms are lifeless, flat
red plates cross-hatched with cracks.
Creosote bleeds its scent.
Soapweed melts. Wherever we look,
dust rises, powdering the dead
and dying leaves of brief spring.

Wherever we look,
any romance of the past
eludes us: we see uncounted hours
of measuring, mapping inclines in memory,
channeling dry earth
and lining those channels with bricks—
a legacy of work, against heat
and drought, natural failures,
lost only in the sleep of arid shade,
the cool purity of dream.

Now crumbling adobe
wavers in the dry afternoon.
Piped water flows warm and chlorine
into our parched mouths.
The monotone sun does not stop.
Finally we climb into cars hot as kilns
and speed smoothly away,
dreaming blank landscape,
a shower, a tall glass of ice,
never ourselves Indian, native,
alive under this blue waste of sky.

1492 Fremont

This begins with a car: four doors,
a boxy, tan sedan, the back
curbside tire flat, the water-stained
rear deck curling naugahyde and
atomized foam, the dash lemon
lime loop carpet, one hubcap gone,
the other watered dull amber
by dogs. The gray, spiteful woman
in 106, the corner unit,
looks at this car whenever she
turns on the water or opens her
kitchen curtains.
        It could be she
curses that car and what collects
under it—the stiff cellular
plastic of fast food packaging,
scroungy cats, the Jennell kids' stuck
foursquare ball. We consider it,
if at all, like landscape, something
there, like her, local, mildly strange.

Because the mail is delivered
at aluminum keyboxes,
one formidable structure also
at the corner, we are aware
she watches. We wave (our pity
is boundless and impersonal)
as we circle that derelict
Buick, if it is not raining.
We cannot be sure we see her
past that glass, confused as it is
by our reflected selves waving.

We cannot be sure why that one
July evening she left the white
doorway (yellow dishwashing gloves,
a pail of white suds, chamois,

and some sort of vermillion scarf
or handkerchief around her hair),
settled before the failing chrome
and began, in no hurry, to
cleanse that object: grille, aerial,
hood and latch, door, door, fender, light,
every window. Superhuman
in this new vision, she pried one
outside hubcap, washed it, replaced
it, not where it had been, but where,
from her kitchen, it would be seen...

At that, our first address, amid
the clutter of dinner (napkins,
milky glasses), door stopped open,
amazed, we watched her work that car
small square by small square, restoring
lustre, like polishing silver.

Fairmoor

Go back and the pebbled concrete
welcomes your heavier steps, dwarf
apples still bearing in the shade.
Long ago three carpets of strawberries
died in compost. The deodar cedar
has risen on its second trunk, and scrub
jays still roost on the phone's high wires.
Every year is smaller. Every year's return
a larger catalog of loss, less interest
in the landscape it contains.

White magnolia thicken near the garage.
August tomatoes climb their steel enclosures
and leggy roses still siren the aphids.
Your brother owns his home. Your parents,
retired, stay healthy and welcome your children:
today this is the yard they play in, eager
stories compelling your attention.
Fairmoor's no dream. Go back,
the upstairs rooms are always empty,
the past forever closing its one door.

Arrival

Nothing is changed:
the kitchen linoleum glows,
heart philodendron twine the hung brass chains.
No one is in the house. Nothing is changed.
Nothing is changed. Round low mahogany
hovers between flowering chairs.
Black, veined marble waits the fire.
Known books, the Edinburgh clock,
and that nameless Grecian copy
(where did she, years ago, come from?)—
nothing's changed.

*

Why do I expect echoes?
Sun slants in on the french prints.
Two dressers and a chiffonier
contain their accustomed clothes.
It is earlier than I wished, or later.
Air says something familiar.
I know the rounded window
and the worn runner on the stair.
I'll find brick stands on brick and stays,
light filling muslin curtains,
the oval table set.

*

I climb from the car.
Boxwood and roses trim the yard.
Transvaal daisies bloom crimson, salmon.
My brother, my parents are there.
We greet each other
not as we are but as we were.

Parochial

Airy as five barns,
timbers hand-hewn, 10 x 15's
and lag bolts thick as pipes.
The glued, dovetailed lattice
of the cloistered choir loft
beyond the wide rectangle
of sanctuary, empty cry room,
the altar with its sealed, saintly relics
and one endless natural candle
burning, hung in its brass sling.

Sweaty, noisy, we'd sneak in at recess,
trying to breathe quiet after kickball.
Mostly we'd just stand inside
the second set of towering double doors,
dust floating, sun down in separate bars,
envelopes and those little pencils,
yellow, sharpened, there for the taking.

Shirts untucked, we looked,
maybe walked a little up a side aisle,
one of the lucent windows cranked open
over camellias, lawn out there,
a Shell station across the street,
somebody's mother's yellow sedan pulling in,
tires over the black cords ringing the bells.

Furniture

Again, tonight, to whatever we call
home, we'll go back, to our potted palms
and philodendron scaling the ceiling,
to our dogs and cats with their numbered
lives and familiar attendant smells.
We'll find circulars and unpaid dunnings
on the hall table exactly as we left them.
The television's dull gray face will neither
announce nor accuse. Perhaps
the telephone rings and we go out again.
Perhaps we find the late afternoon light
something we had not known we'd
forgotten—how it illumines Aunt Loretta's
sway-back settee, its balding, burgundy
velveteen testimony to a long, historical
decline. Nine nights out of ten,
that is the dream.

One night, never sought or planned,
it's all wrong: uncommon traffic, a small
cluster of neighbors who go too quickly
silent. And no wonder, for beyond them
the obscene orange and magenta flames
are all there is. In this dream, no one
burns. The dog's in shock and whines,
its fur wet. In the blistered garage,
on a high dusty rafter, the cat watches
and will not come down. All night it stays
with the turpentine and the oiled tools.
Outside, what else is there to do but stand
on the seared lawn and watch the lifetime
of fire. Some nights I lie down
on a suddenly strange bed, and cannot
sleep. For a long time the air
is noisy, a red moon neon and flashing,

and I am afraid of dreaming, afraid
of that hysteria of waking smoke-blind,
choking on the dry powder of ash,
desperate for my family, desperate
to know what, if anything, can be saved.

Flood Waters

Standing behind Venetian blinds,
He's looking or not looking
At a slick, uneven street,
Unrusted rails down its middle,
Rainwater, a line of parked
Pickups and sedans.

Or he's behind the desk,
Mail slit open, sorted and read,
Phone lights unlit. He's thinking
Of numbers, flood waters, Engine 31
Waxed and cherry red, river
Rising on its hubs, pumps noisy,
And the basement a still, dark lake
Under the chrome flashlight.
He's thinking heart attacks, that commotion
Of gray-blue skin, minutes and sirens
And the air sharper, meaning something.
Drunks under empty freight cars,
Union Pacific, Cotton Belt, the Great
Northern goat—chick peas
Still rattling in the sideboards—
Chick peas or bulk rice or soybeans like bearings.
At this dead end of autumn, he's thinking
Summer, the warehouse like an open oven
Even at 8 a.m. when chain doors
Roll overhead and the day,
Deep blue, begins.

It's the slow afternoon before a holiday,
Before a ritual meal, his sons and daughter
Grown, their strangeness, and their children
and their dolls. The dolls have names.
Whatever he thinks of, it's not at all
Like time, none of it over or complete.
It's late. Maybe at this point
He puts on his raincoat.
Dusk and frost settle as he drives, radio
On, and low clouds scour the moon.

This Hour

In the unremodeled lounge,
someone dead now is singing,
        guessing at weddings and birthdays,
ignoring the bare tables.
Two people sit happy in that lounge,
              the St. Francis,
San Francisco, first week in May, 1947.
Outside it is unusually clear.
            They never go outside,
never imagine they could have.

*

Once I walked into my mother's kitchen,
her feet propped in the warming oven,
        GAS WORKS EXPLOSION
a front-page gray fireball
        on the paper she held.
I knew the word gas and said it out loud,
Gas. She lowered the paper.
          On Sunday afternoons
my father's Blitz beer bottle
mysteriously gathered water to its brown side,
          ringing the shaded table.
Ring and ring and ring,
        I held the bottle,
tasted the cold, delicious bitterness of all adults.

*

Tonight I see my father slumped and asleep,
          breathing noisily
the cigarette air of his sweater.
It's not likely he sees that morning
       his own father's cancerous death
made of the tatted curtains lies,
          dusted ancient bannisters

all dull shine reconstructed in dream.
Nor does he see that oddly empty parking space,
                              his '54 buick stolen,
port-holed blue sides humming somewhere
in monotonous drizzle,
recovered days later,
                              dry coat on the dry seat,
beside a stale loaf of Bernhart's unsliced rye.

*

Are you going to bed?
                    No answer.
Upright, determined, my mother
examines the *Sunset* recipes,
counting times, tasting and judging.
                              Or she reads.
The evening goes.
                    And whatever my father hears—
sports, weather, my mother in the next room washing—
it all tells him as in a dream
                    go to bed.
The stovelight's black, screendoor locked.
Drawn curtains make of the half moon a blur.

*

Whatever they must remember and save unspoken
is no burden in the simple evening.
Daylight escapes them and disappears.
                              When I was small,
they brushed their teeth with powders.
At this hour,
              one turns off the lamp
and in the close and familiar dark,
          they lie down, my mother and father,
              my mother and my father.

The Biographer's Art

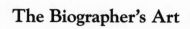

Postcard

It was all true now because it happened
to him as he wrote...

He wanted to say something about Hemingway,
the daily business of emotion
and its evasions. What he wanted to say
was not local, as newspapers were once local.
It had nothing centrally to do
with weather, though weather was part of it.
He wanted to say emotion was location:
the life of numbered houses, mapped bodies of water.
He wanted to say emotion was food, or, better,
drink—champagne, say, or Pernod, impossible Basque wine
swallowed for the glorious, romantic fact of itself.

Whatever he said had to be surer, clearer than that.
Something about Hemingway, the wide picture of his face
inflated by emotion, illness, drink.
Something about the literal man he had met once,
nodded to on the snow-crunching road.
A man bearded, briefly polite with his face:
The man he had turned and watched walk
briskly into the flurries of a late Idaho afternoon.

Child

—after a *Smithsonian* photograph.

Dead, or old past memory,
you would recognize this figure
—gaunt hands, black stained nails,
the one eye in profile bloodshot
even in black and white—
only typical of what you knew:

children six years of age professional
thieves, not of food or cash,
but coal, some literal
warmth to live by (1918, New York
colder than Fairbanks, and all coal
gone for the war—
dying here or there an equal event).

No longer yourself, it can be said
you're clean now of that coal dust,
that particular squalor of conscience,
my own and the world's.
Here, all feeling
is history, hence useless.
I think of your parents

who, if they loved you, hurt,
and seeing you, hated themselves.

Vermeer: *The Music Lesson*

"the domain of music is time; that of painting is space"
—*Rousseau*.

A room in late medieval clothing:
oak ceiling beams
frame the far plaster wall;
the diamond checkered floor
leads us to a table, a white water pitcher,
a partially hidden chair.

Beyond these and the blond *viola de gamba*,
there is a Flemish virginal, a girl
standing at the keys, her back to us,
the blouse of her dress lit by afternoon
diffusing through glass windows to our left.

Elegantly long haired,
(we'd call him affected in attire
—lace, a white linen sash across his chest—)
her music master stands to her right, listening,
watching perhaps now her hands, now her face.

The virginal's case is open like a tomb,
the latin inscription: *Musica Laetitae Comes
Medicina Dolorum*, music accompanies joy,
eases sorrow.

The girl's dress falls in straight folds
the dark blue of ground lapis.
Hair gathered and pinned up,
only ringlet sidecurls touch her ears.
We are as we always are.
Unknown music fills the room.

Waiting For Nothing

Tom Kromer, American Century Series

No name inside.
$4.65 penciled in a corner, crossed out.
Three dollars and forty cents buys me this book.

Memory confusion between us,
my father, class of 1932,
posted stock quotations. Minimum wage,
chamois and chalk on slate walls,
numbers and numbers and numbers.

The dedication, not as I thought I remembered,
not Sally, But Jolene. "For Jolene,
who turned off the gas." Yellow houses,
he says, yellow but not too yellow:
food, and never turned away.
A thousand such houses.
The spectacle of a man living on one color.

In my childhood, on the fritz meant
not working: anything, animate or not,
broken, needing repair. The silver-side
chrome toaster, heavy, swollen as a bubble
and cold as stone.

Out of hunger and the urge to forget it,
Norman Rockwells are born.
Haydn's 56th Sonata circles under a needle.
This is the luxury of reading, of not reading.

Harbor

—after Winslow Homer.

You cannot tell if it is afternoon.
Outside, beached hulls slant on mudflats
that steam in raw winter, the harbor and its hills
fogged suggestions in the gunmetal distance.
You cannot tell when the boatmen
in great boots and heavy oilskin coats
might return, leaving the etched glass
of their 19th century steins,
the short flights of darts into brown cork.
Perhaps all the long hours of that shrouded afternoon
they stay inside, alternately sullen,
explosive with laughter,
the Wellington clock dependable in its announcements.
And perhaps they welcome the unspoken observation
the harbor never clears, a day fogged inside and out.

Boots off, men line the bar.
One, made smaller by perspective, has already
passed out, slumped beyond an emptied glass.
The oak fire roars; the dog
sleeps as peacefully as stars, unnoticed
and oblivious to all human noise—
the arguing over family or weather, anything
but the catch, which has been good,
and the dead, too many, useless to speak of.
Slowly the black piers recede.
By now many of the men have drained a last stein,
pulled on their boots, and gone
to their wives, children, the table
with its familiar grain and porcelain.
Lit in the bar's wavy mirror, the few remaining boatmen

sing like deranged Protestants,
loudly and from memory, their words slurring
on the night's thick air.

Outside, windows are the dark's only moons.
Twice the sea has filled the harbor's chambers.
Beyond the light of an open door, the anchored hulls
are there, refloated, chains slack in the calm.
Patient, empty with possibility,
they rise and fall.

The Biographer's Art

All identity is active statement.
—*George Steiner.*

What is your substance, whereof are you made?
—*Shakespeare.*

1.

A file of dated letters and a voice,
the important survivor agrees at last
to your visit, two days for your recorder.
What you know, you review, earliest
meetings, estrangements, awkward returnings,
rumors and echoes of rumors, questions,
a desire to breathe that air.

Finally hours of the luxury of listening,
conversation an exhausting, vibrant monologue.

2.

Breath and weather, the brick garden wall,
there is no one life. There is no one life
except as it is imagined, imagined in its own time,
imagined now, slowly, in the fact of your work.

No tomb or conversation
carries the impact of Hollinger boxes
catalogued, under lock and key,
subject to permission.

Letters, fragments of memoirs,
records, reports—you move among them,
time like water overhead, dull color,
impossible eels and eyeless fish—

they do not contradict,
neither do they agree.
In the life beside your own, yarrow
blossoming, spun cotton drying on the lines.

A sail on the horizon. 2 p.m.

3.

Hours of acedia, pencil on the desk

coffee in a cup, ash-tray flowing
the window closed, the universe unforthcoming,
Being ground to a halt—

To characterize one person clearly
requires the habits of character.
Maybe you just try to sleep,

one yellowed letter replaying itself like memory:

"Arrived yesterday flat-out defeated by
distance, by that necessary requirement every
fact of our lives be continued on faith,
disassembled, boxed, in transit or rented storage.
See how tired we are: everything's melodrama!
One Mrs. Ruth Hayes stopped over with a bag of ripe
Macintosh apples. The house, which fondly we'd thought
of as a collection of adjectives, has become a
solid array of nouns: ash flooring in the kitchen,
and delightfully grotesque jungle birds all the
way up the stairwell. Upstairs, we crank
the windows open and the Milky Way is also
a collection of nouns. We sleep to crickets,
awaken to astounding disorder waiting for
something to occur. The icebox has, at least,
a pitcher of juice. No one mentioned the backyard
was all Star of David, hydrangea, white lilacs…"

4.

The chief feature of the landscape, and of your
life in it, was the air.
                              —*Isak Dinesen*.

Like Stevens's "Planet,"
bound galleys on the table;
you have written a new version
of yourself—that place and texture
faithful at last, at least to the chosen
photographs, one glossy paper signature:

the infant propped on the stone wall;

the parents' separate portraits
somber as time exposure;

one, later, subject informal, solo
before the lily pool—water and blooms
past depth of focus, shimmering, the white-
washed house wall in endless dissolve;

one walking; one formal for awards;

the hat photo (face dark in its shade),
friends bored or distracted or slightly drunk
on a long afternoon of alcohol and air—

5.

> What a curious relation is mine with Roger at this
> moment—I who have given him a kind of shape after
> his death. Was he like that? I feel very much in
> his presence at the moment; as if I were intimately
> connected with him: as if we together had given birth
> to this vision of him: a child born of us. Yet he
> had no power to alter it. And yet for some years it
> will represent him.
> —*Virginia Woolf.*

Picture a breakfast table,
toast with strawberry preserves,
coffee steaming in a red porcelain cup,
an endless procession of red hens
fired around its side.
The stranger becomes you,
becomes you as you write,
as you believe.
No stranger exits, though someone does,

*—there is another extract or two—one especially which I will copy
tomorrow—for the candles are burnt down and I am using the wax
taper—which has a long snuff on it—the fire is at its last click—I
am sitting with my back to it with one foot rather askew upon the
rug and the other with the heel a little elevated from the carpet—I
am writing this on the Maid's tragedy which I have read since tea
with Great pleasure—Besides this volume of Beaumont &
Fletcher—there are on the table two volumes of Chaucer and a new
work of Tom Moores called Tom Cribbs memorial to
Congress—nothing in it—These are trifles—but I require nothing so
much of you as that you will give me a like description of yourselves
however it may be as you are writing to me—*

the web and intricacies
of a personal history, a natural life:
there it is, here are you.
The bonds slacken or calcify or metamorphose—

they remain. Biography begins its own existence.
In that brief condition
of absence, moments arrive
without ceremony or design,

a positive amnesia of nouns—
cantaloupe and ripening plums,
lover, hair wet and darker,
a child swinging, a neighbor
opening a door. No sense of
beginning or of ending.
No ambition beyond embrace.

Walkers

House

The ice in his highball glass clinked
as he lifted it—the familiar, watery scotch.
Odd, he thought, the day's like a skin,
like that translucent, scaly sleeve
airy on a dry bed of juniper. He'd sawn that bush
at its base (years ago now), wrestled it
into the wheelbarrow, and finally up
onto the tan tailgate,
the wheelbarrow idiotically light, bouncing
empty as he walked it back
to that circle of brown, brittle and spiky twigs
where the juniper had been, where he'd found that skin,
four, five inches long, unmoved,
hollow in the windless air.
Gently he'd slid his last finger into it
and held it up, astonished.
It did not crumble or disappear—
it warmed his finger, gave it an odd color.
I wonder what happened to that...
He set down the glass.

Her mother's before her,
already in her keeping these 35 years,
she treasured the French cutlery,
its heft and delicate balance,
pearl, steel, the easy motion of its cutting.
She was watching the blade where it glinted,
seeing the small grinding wheel
nubbed and uniformly dense with its freckled grit,
all blurred when the low, wound motor spun it smooth,
one color. She'd layed the knives on the counter,

no particular order, but all of them,
may as well make it pay.
And something always jumped a little
when she touched the blade to that wheel—
sparks, the sudden noise
something to ignore, careful of the angle
as the edge emerged visibly brightened,
yesterday's comics page slowly
but surely sliced into streamers.
Maybe her head *was* still ringing a little.

Television off and the upright Philco,
one overhead light on, another through the open
pocket door—on the stage of their dining room,
its ornate black mirror and shellacked dark furniture,
they are eating supper. Walking by,
you might wonder what they're saying—
his sagged chin, the ropy veins of her hands.
You might think to ask after their children
or wonder at them as children—
the smaller, smoother bodies they were.
Or perhaps we are their children
and they are talking about us
as they move towards the wide window
to look out again: empty street, black trees,
black hawthornes, predictable stars.
Maybe they're agreeing, making a last point
as he stands there, hands in baggy pockets,
as she moves just out of sight
and pulls the curtains closed.

Zuelke's

Foam white and green in the swells,
blinding in the noon sun of our arrival
as the children run away from us
ignorant of the north Pacific cold,

how can this be the same ocean
any of us knew years ago,
binoculars like weights in our hands
as we tried to steady freighters in our gaze?
When I remember that room,
I see one wall entirely glass,
forgetting, as I did then, the meal
on a rose Franciscan plate—turkey, white
potatoes, dead and liquid peas.
I ignore the difficult conversation
of those adults, the grandparents
I love with timeless nonchalance:
Do they notice how out there
surf layers towards us
five and sometimes six deep
even as we sit here,…
the glimmer, dazzle, and shine
at last an explosion behind seared eyes.

When the children touch water
their mouths open, shocked surprise
one with the general roar.
We're here as we've forgotten we are,
landscape declaring itself,
the sea an ocean of weather.

After Drought

After a morning of clouds
nudging and backing up pale gray against dark hills,
ground hard as linoleum
and the rain, blessed, draining into cracks
deeper than a pencil, there's that imagined sigh
of land asked too long to hold its breath.
After that, after some similar morning,
you hear yourself say something like
"You're lovely," or "Darling,"
and wonder whose odd voice you're hearing,
whose clothing you've borrowed or will borrow this time.

What about the screaming of children, ours,
who have, awake, almost no reason
for terror—where have they
learned fear at any hour?
Remember your father's shirts, starched,
four to each blue box, WHITE CLEANERS,
and fastened with that twine he snapped once
angry, too angry to trust what he might say
against the kitchen and its silence,
collars slamming into the dresser drawer,
the muscles of his arm, cuffs rolled back,
white against tan?

What about the face and long body
you lay with in what must be,
sometimes, ecstasy? What about the once
or twice we settle back like feathers,
entirely benign colonizers
of bone and actual room?
After drought, hills announce a color.
Blink and blink, we're back.
"Darling," or, "You're lovely."

Noise

This is the hour of mass murder. Hear
it? The sound of physics. The soft, breath-
less whir of the atom.
                          —*Tim o'Brien*

No he says to himself,
it's not that,
not, at 2:38 in the dark morning,
anything but hail, iceballs

pearly under the switched floodlight,
bouncing on the lawn, on concrete,
on the aging cedar overhead.

Mouth open, Beth sleeps in a drum.
You could sing in here
and not wake her, not hear yourself sing.

Her sister has kicked all blankets off.
She stretches and grinds her teeth,
a syndrome I knew the name of once,
a noise audible over the lessening roar.

2:52 and their half-roused mother
rolls over, "Where've you been?"
The bed's warm near her.
Water's noisy in the gutters.
The ceiling's a deep, impossible blur.

Fathers and Infants

On 17 separate screens—
I counted them between rounds—Carl
"The Truth" Williams jabs and jabs, slips
the Holmes' right, shakes his head no,
that knockdown in the third an earlier lifetime,
seconds and minutes adding up as we watch,
bell and commercial simultaneous and loud.
They're pushing beer, and it pours colder there
than it ever is, cold, pure, and by the time the song
is half done, we're most of us looking down
the White Sale aisle or maybe watching the escalator stairs
rise and slide flat under the seamless floor.
My Jason's sound asleep, the Nuk still stuck
in his slack mouth. Rosy around the lips,
he's still breathing, buckled in his layback stroller.
Radios, stereo-chairs, the big projection TV
with its half-size, pale screen—this
is Home Entertainment in the anchor store.
Lingerie is one floor up, with dresses, the beauty parlor.
Next door is Appliances, four spendy rows
of energy efficient, no fingerprint freezers,
refrigerators, dishwashers—your Whirlpools and
Maytags—even trash compactors somebody wants.
Downstairs it's donuts, a snackbar in the economy basement.

This guy belonging to a plaid umbrella stroller,
his daughter in a blue dress and matching bonnet, says
"Look at Holmes. 35. He's fat."
Fat or not, right now his one fight's a measured ring,
Everlast right cocked like a hammer, and his cheek

swollen, like it's overstuffed with cotton.
The anonymous daughter in the plaid stroller
(I'd call her Rebecca on account of the bonnet),
she pats her soft knees, open palms up and down,
up and down, her legs kicking too—all of her
bouncing so insistent the stroller wheels
roll back and forth in the carpet dents.
The bell again, beer, or cars, something
MADE THE AMERICAN WAY. Soccer crowds riot…
Reagan… Nicaragua… News Digest…
Rebecca's rubbing her eyes with her fists.
Was it five years ago Boom Boom Mancini
killed that guy—Korean. I saw the round on tape—
nothing like this fight. Four days
I prayed for Benny Kid Paret, for all the good
it did him or my fifth grade parochial soul.
Listen, the kids are all asleep, except Rebecca
and she's just cooing with every punch.
Six of us here, counting the sales guy, each of us

thirsty, each of us sure we need a new truck.
Jason's out like a light. Then his mother's back,
a kiss for us both, packages under one arm.
So we're turning, ready to stroll towards Parking,
and I see Ali standing second row ringside,
grinning, waving a towel over his head.
He knows a sad fight when he sees one.
Ali, Ali, Ali, Ali, you can read his chanting lips
and the crowd's with him. He's leading his own cheers.

Power Outage

Nearly 8:40 by the battery clock, sky
cloudy, some distant, cawing crows,
and all the room's light's ancient,
Flemish, say. Not quite Vermeer's,
but natural, the soft shadows of morning.

Saturday, and somebody's errant
car is the probable cause of all this,
the bumper *recessed*—a polite, even genteel
way to say it—the long black synthetic
and chrome still rusted a little,

still parking-lot dented, now an arrow
through the radiator's green and leaky heart.
The creosote pole's splintered ten feet
above impact, swaying and held
by phone lines, the frayed power

like a sparkler six inches over the paving.
Crows gone, not one music video
or weather channel, at such a pleasant,
easy hour, someone—woman if that's you,
or man—you round a corner in an old Bel Aire, say,

wing windows open, and so what
if the upholstery's going. Up ahead
you see that pole at its new angle,
the stopped, utterly silent car. You
brake. Stop. Open your door, climb out,

(door ajar behind you, dome light burning),
and you walk over, afraid, maybe even
praying against what you hope
isn't there—the windshield spidery
as some medieval painting, and nothing

but a half-bald corpse slumped in dead, ugly color.
It's not that bad, some moaning,
and the light's coming back on!
Faint music from some other room.
It's time for a deep breath.

Somewhere along the line, you started
to read the paper. 9:15. In the minutes
since you looked up, your first grader
measured, cut, tied, glued, and named
an entire family of yarn dolls.

Or you were alone, the house
still in every circuit, something about crows,
and for awhile you forgot entirely who
and where you were. Which now seems
terrifying, but wasn't then: it was pleasant.

July At the 45th Parallel

The sun is out and it is a beautiful day.
Saying things like that means
we're here, sort of. Something pleasant
and vague and meant not to cause much
reflection. It works. The sun is out,

we're drunk in canvas chairs,
and up the road a brown city police car
has stopped a woman in a purple Chrysler
Le Baron. She's flustered, her hair
just done, tinted the red/brown

of an Irish setter, and now this.
It's because Brian Moore, a total stranger,
a kid, rode his bike into traffic—
big news, front page sad news in a town
this size, and she feels guilty the red lights

caught her, and angry, the hair appointment
later than she'd planned, the day hotter.
The reporter who covered the Brian Moore tragedy
was touched, genuinely, or not touched.
He went to the funeral to see

the family, other kids, the cemetery
with presumably all those other stories. He wrote
a nice column about feelings. But right about
now the woman is signing her ticket,
thinking maybe there's already more

than enough aimless grief in the air
this beautiful day, even if her own life
is pretty much patched up, rinsed, the right
color. And isn't it just bad timing anyway,
that this Moore kid should ride

off that sidewalk then, only two weeks ago? And her
car be air conditioned, the day hot, her windows
up, radio on, and the engine as quiet as
Idaho at night, no sense of speed,
that cop cleverly hidden and polite?

She smiles at his sunglasses, says
thank you, such forced manners, stuffs
the ticket into the glovebox, glances
at the mirror, lights revolving like obscenities,
the cop writing something

and what her foot really wants to do is
stomp on it, bicycles or no bicycles.
Brain Moore's dead. That's too bad.
There's not one thing under heaven anyone can
do for him. The air comes back on with a rush.

When she shifts, the wheels
lurch a little. She's thinking
She'll put the state registration
back in its leather visor holder later.
And she's reaching for her sunglasses

as the Chrysler slides away, maples
overhead, gravel popping under the Goodyears.

Indulgence

This evening only electricity
dictates that clock tick its quartz
regularity there beyond the open
casement all the time we slouch
in patio chairs on the concrete veranda.
Just now the conversation has been
full of hypothetical figures—memory,
conjectures of memory, relations
long deceased, lilacs, the clock
which continues, the alternate loudness
of automobiles passing, then the wide
macadam warm in its vacant lassitude.
For awhile, it all stays quiet,
maples gently respiring, the late air
so blessedly full we may remain
stuporous and dull, not gazing
at anything, or each other.
No sires wail. No blazing porchlights
compel the battered moths.
Out there, vast acres of inaction
unlit by any houses.
Down our street, one cardiac sprinkler
steadily soaking a parched lawn.

Blue

A woman ironing.
Maybe she is saying something up there
as the shirts smooth.
Maybe she whistles the same
six note melody,
as the long, padded board creaks,
rickety on its folding legs,
as starch and steam warm the air,
and towels and napkins and washcloths
tumble in the round, hot window.

Outside, when she reaches up,
her heels rise. She's clothes-pinning
everything in the sodden basket—
white socks, underwear, handkerchiefs,
and large percale rectangles, three sides
hung damp from the umbrella lines.
Inside that white enclosure, he watches her
smile as the last sheet unfolds, as her hands
crimp it with blankfaced, woodenheaded
pins, there, there, and disappear.
He watches her shoes
walk away.

Left inside that square, white
and dirty clouds in strange motion as he watches,
the child fears for the blooming roses,
even the thorns which, peeled from their stems,
will stick to skin. He fears
for the parsley, for the double windows
and the back door.
He thinks they may be a vaporous dream.

Sleeping or not, he screams. Methodical,
frowning, he inhales another profound breath.
He is screaming louder than white
and he has mostly closed his eyes.

When one white corner opens like a door,
his mother pins it there,
her mouth and the lines at her brows
laughing as she lifts him up
to the curve of her shoulder
and the smell of her hair.
It never occurs to him he might forget this.

He turns his head: white
lines and clothespins, past them
arborvitae, blue spruce, phonewires, blue.

City of Roses

1. Air

Here in a white and mechanical room suffused
With respiration and clotted with burning tears

As a surgical tube trickles urine into a collection bag
Slung on a hook at the foot of a steel bed,

5:10 on a Tuesday afternoon in July
(Blankly, without seeing it,

I have been staring at that tube
Where it snakes out yellow from under sheets),

Here among relatives and a family of technical strangers,
Dying is not a little or mean or cheap thing.

Nothing prepares for this, no memory, argument,
Fragment of whistled song or unfinished story—

Nothing prepares for this. Futile, nowhere to go,
I look at a slack, half-lidded face

And want to fix its color. I want to argue with monitors,
Their fluctuations and banal numbers.

Neither do the hands grasp nor the eyes see.
the corneas are healthy, we sign the papers.

All this seriousness, weariness—
I want to laugh like a child ten minutes into the sermon.

And I want to swear to you the soul rises.
It mingles on the air

With a hopeful buoyancy beyond my ability to credit.
For a little while, it mingles on the air.

We breathe it in, we breathe it out,
For a little while.

2. Another Summer

Two seasons later
he said the summer
resembled a home movie
alternately soft focus and dreamy,
hazy like that skyline
from the brow of the hill
where after the interment they'd stood
dumbstruck and lightheaded as poultry—

that or a grainy documentary
replaying as the projector jerks and clicks,
as the respirator in the gray picture
whirs its oxygen air
stopping and starting and stopping.
You take one breath, another,
another—he'd written that to someone,
one of those letters weepy with truth.

The truth is, two seasons later
his mother inhabits his dreams.
In one the sunshine's amber, 1940's,
after the war. Every Chevrolet
is a monument to victory and to chrome.
She's waved her hair. The radio announcer
is Arthur Godfrey before his cancer.
She's outside on the porch swing

he's known only in pictures.
Sit down, his mother says, a voice normal as rain,
We're the same age.
The porch swing creaks. She gazes
at a lily pool, black and orange carp mouthing the water.
She curls on the seat; she rests her head.
I enjoy these dreams.
Sometimes they go on and on

like afternoons blue
with tropical clouds, lily blossoms,
red geraniums, honeysuckle...
And as she speaks, as she falls gently asleep,
he is thinking this is my mother,
a woman almost a girl.
The afternoon sun warms her like a drug.
She's waved her hair.

3. The Indeterminate Hours

> I want to begin with rain.
> —*Tess Gallagher*

Rain, evening, the earlier hours
are anger and pleasure without memory.
A woman pauses at the door.
Her manner, and whatever she says,
are as familiar as the house itself.
Something about dreams as she closes that door.
Something about funny papers, tomorrow,
as light narrows, the child
already breathing in even cadence.

If I know that house, the hallway
and carpet and door,
if I know the child sleeps
and if I know the child's dreams,
the woman must be younger than I remember.
She must be my mother.

I know the rain: it begins later,
an indeterminate hour.
It begins softly and wakes no one
until finally the downspouts are throaty
and the clock face is phosphor green
and its black hands
make circle after circle
leisurely and with a low hum.

4. April

A woman I knew later
is humming, exactly. Smoking.
She has folded the daily paper back
half, then quarter,
and she leans on a tile counter.
Outside, on a picnic table near the back door,
a bucket of gray ammonia water
sits by a pile of wrung, damp rags.
April, midweek, and she has worked that morning
washing storm windows. Rinsed and drying,
they rest under sills and mirror
rhododendrons, cherry boughs, white
gutters and eaves. She has made coffee
and the sun refracts the steam
as it curls, rises. She is
reading crosswords, humming,
yellow pencil lettering the squares.

5. City of Roses

In a hospital room with an already forgotten number,
though a parent's body stops—the respirator useless,
though survivors weep
or walk unaffected and dazzled down carpeted halls,
at home, inside, nothing moves, nothing alters.
Not that bird streak on the high window,
not the blackened, gray fireplace,
the hammered brass, round, ornamental relief,
nor the refrigerator's steel-slatted shelves—
mustard, sweet midgets, creme cheese, Best Foods.
Whirlpool. The chill, unspoiled wealth of produce.

As again surely it will,
on this, a day of unspeakable beauty,
the significant, the real end comes.
A day of roses—tropicanas, Mr. Lincolns,
granadas, shastas—a day
brilliant with early August sun and nothing happening,
no trauma, no untoward emotion.
The floral curtains hold light
and shade as they have for years.
Automated solicitations occupy the phone lines; they hum.
A gentle wind stirs the upright hawthorne.
Sooner or later grief arrives at this juncture

and stops or evaporates or ...
The robins don't care, nor the musical towhees, coast pines,
the garden's stolid path of river rock concrete.
For days, at work or commuting, windows down,
radio on, we are not occupied with matter,
how it is cold at the core, hot first, then cold.
But, praise us, we are not.
We are morose, we are euphoric, we are plural.
The alarm clock burrs and we shut it off.
And the backyard birch makes small applause
and the roses, the cities of roses, squint in that light.
They nod under opulent burdens
of fragrance and of color through breakfast
and forever into August.

All Day the Sea

West beyond wish or confusion, the continent
ends: sand islands, riffles and pocket lakes,
steamy fog swirling over eel grass
and beach peas, distant breakers in sunlight
a merging definition of white. Here landscape
and language are the same: the brine-stiff
articulate sleeves of ocean tubers and stalks,
file dogwinkles and doveshells, crab debris—
pincers and the tipped, shallow bowls—the anonymous
polished remains of trees.

                         All day the sea
is the sky, its darker color, gulls aloft
on bare rumors of wind. All day with no
sensation of motion, we turn slowly, the planetary
turning, until the low sun's glare burns
a corridor on the water-glazed beach.
Amber and deep red ride the horizon's clouds;
barges crawl south, wavering lights
in an ocean of black sound. All evening
salt fires warm our houses, low stars
numerous in their bright sockets. All night
a chorus washes over us in the dark—salt air,
salt air and the constant tide.

Walkers

On a normal morning,
sunshine, the recent arrival
of acrobatic tree swallows,
the heart explodes pain, volcanic,
paralysis of arms and chest.
It quivers, a reed
vibrating and blurred in the stiff breeze
which has filled the office
or the garage. It seizes up
and slowly begins to cool.
Felled by it, terrified, aching,
what must be the emotions
resuming, stricken but regular,
the weightless room settling in gravity?

Afterwards, after medication
and the necessary unnecessary cautions,
after the conscious odd surgery of balloons,
or the grafting, replumbing, ribs
pried open with a vise,
everything sacred exposed to air,
to vision, and rearranged,
repacked during a long black
and vacant dream—afterwards,
clothed again, only family or friends
find the changes obvious and wonder
how much should be said, or how little.
After it is safe to stand,
after the new diet is habit
and sleeping and waking and breathing
are normal, harmless, it is time
to walk, daily, in the old sense *religiously*.

We pass them on sidewalks
as we fumble with the car's radio
or change gears. We see them
rounding the corner at the top

71

of our slight hill, some of them moving
easily as animals, some laboring
and flushed. Maples shed. Rain
darkens the raw afternoons.
They have clothes for any weather.
They walk for the time it takes,
for whatever they see.

ABOUT THE AUTHOR

Lex Runciman was born and raised in the Pacific Northwest and now teaches at Oregon State University in Corvallis. His work has appeared in many periodicals including *Antaeus, Carolina Quarterly, New England Review & Bread Loaf Quarterly,* and *Northwest Review.* He has been editor of *Quarterly West* and is the current editor for Arrowood Books. His first volume of poems, *Luck,* was issued in a limited edition by Owl Creek Press in 1981. He is married and has two children.